A Triangle for Adaora

An African Book of Shapes

IFEOMA ONYEFULU

FRANCES LINCOLN

I'm worried about my little cousin Adaora. She has been behaving strangely. She keeps saying "I really like paw-paw", over and over again.

But when her mother put a slice of paw-paw on Adaora's favourite plate, Adaora just stared at it.

Why won't she eat the paw-paw? If it had been oranges, pineapples or *udala* (a fruit we all love), it would have disappeared very quickly!

One afternoon, I asked Adaora why she wouldn't eat paw-paw.

"Because I don't want to spoil the pretty shape in the middle."

"That's a **star**," I said. "But there are lots of other interesting shapes to look at."

"What shapes?" said Adaora.

"Shapes like – squares ... circles ... triangles."

"I like that word – triangle," said Adaora.

"If I promise to find you one, will you eat up your paw-paw?"

So I searched for a triangle for Adaora. Easier said than done!

 The first shape I found was a **square**. My big sister Uzo was using an *apkasa* to sift grated casava roots for frying.

"Is that a triangle?" asked Adaora.

"No, Adaora. It's a square," I said.

Apkasa

This is a colander made from dried coconut palms, woven into a flat mat and held in a frame of big sticks.

 Then I saw Uncle Eze on his way to see his parents. He was wearing an *agbada*. Uncle Eze likes to show off and when he saw us, he waved his arms in the air.

"Look, Adaora!" I said. "A **rectangle**."

"That's a nice shape," said Adaora.

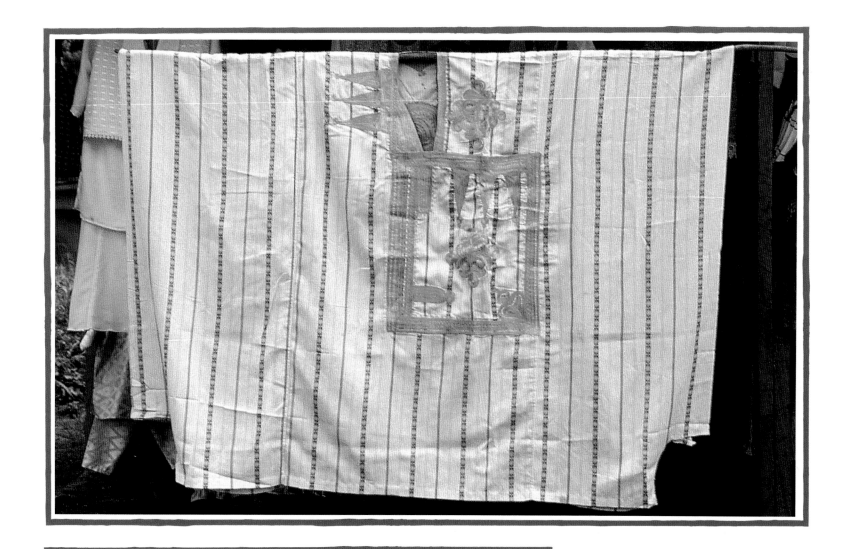

Agbada

This is a beautifully-embroidered robe worn by men for weddings, funerals and many other special occasions.

Suddenly we heard drums playing nearby. We ran towards the sound – and there were four musicians rehearsing for a festival. I love drums, especially big "elephant" drums.

I said to Adaora, "Look at the tops of those drums! Those are **circles**."

The musicians were good. So we listened, and when they had finished playing, we followed them.

Elephant drums

These beat out important news and make special announcements.

We were just turning the corner when I saw a little girl wearing a necklace of cowrie shells.

I pointed at the girl. "Look, Adaora. **Ovals**!"

Adaora stared, and the girl stared back. So we ran off.

Cowrie shells

Many years ago, cowrie shells were used as money, but now we wear them as jewellery, or when we pray for our ancestors.

We turned on to a footpath. Just then, I saw *akwukwo ede* growing nearby.

"Look, **heart** shapes," I said to Adaora. She looked at the leaves for a long time, then agreed that they really were heart-shaped.

"But what about my triangle?" she asked.

Akwukwo ede

We use this plant in our cooking because it is easy to digest. The leaves are wrapped around grated water yam, then steamed and eaten by very young and very old people.

 Where could I find that triangle? I darted about like a butterfly, looking everywhere, until ...

"Adaora, I can see a **diamond**. Come and see."

Across the road, a woman was waiting for a bus. She was wearing a wrapper with a huge diamond printed on the front.

"I like the colours," said Adaora.

Wrappers

These are usually worn by married women, but men wear them, too, on special occasions.

 We walked on down the road. Then I saw two clay bowls on a table.

"Look, Adaora – **semi-circles**! They're for sale, and they look just like the soup bowls we have at home."

"Pity they're not triangles. My feet are getting tired," grumbled Adaora.

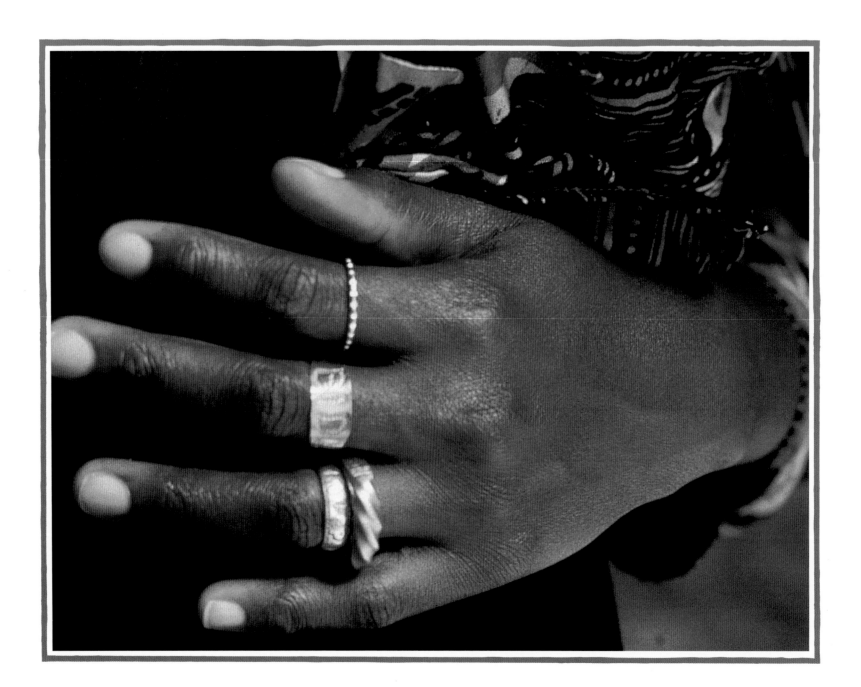

We turned into another road and saw a woman wearing four brass **rings** on her fingers. The middle ring was a special one to show that she was a chief.

"When I grow up, I'm going to wear rings on *all* my fingers!" said Adaora. For a moment she forgot about the triangle and her sore feet.

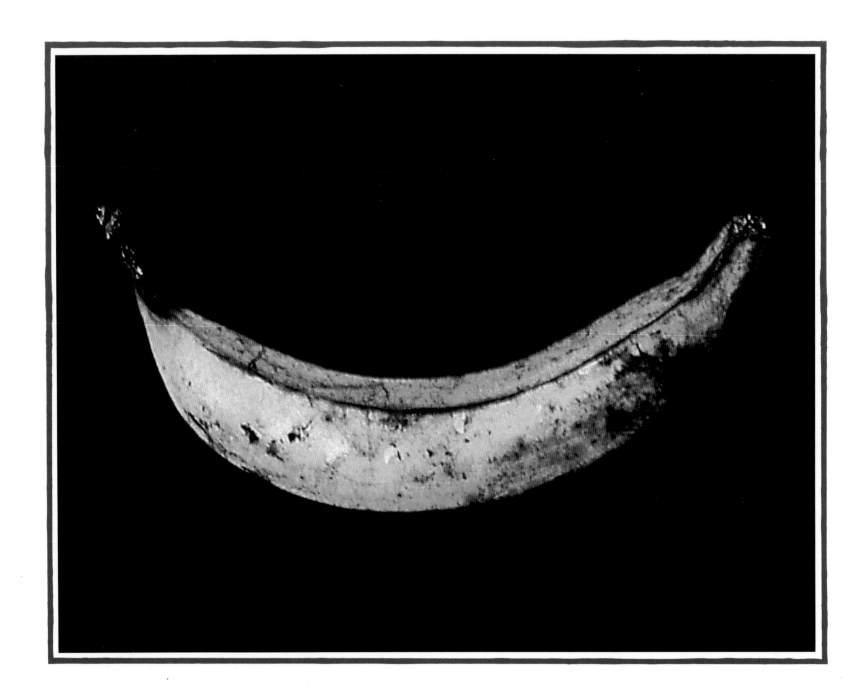

 We walked on. Then I spotted a big plantain. My mouth began to water. "Hey, Adaora!" I said. "There's a **crescent** shape!"

Adaora said, "I'm tired. I want to go home. You don't know what a triangle looks like, anyway."

"Yes I do," I said. "Let's go over there. I can see a big crowd – perhaps there's a festival going on."

Plantains

These look like bananas, but they are vegetables, and we fry or roast them over charcoal fires. They taste good roasted with palm oil and chilli pepper.

 I ran on ahead, pushing between people. But the only shapes I could see were more circles and rectangles. Then suddenly ...

"Look, Adaora – a **triangle**! I told you I'd find one. That woman is wearing the most beautiful headdress I've ever seen. It's like the one my mother made. I watched her tie it up and fix it in place with pins."

Adaora smiled, and clapped her hands. "That's *my* triangle!"

The woman turned round, and said, "Uzo and Adaora! What are you doing so far from home?"

It was Auntie Felicia! She gave us each a big hug, then took us home.

 The next day, Auntie Felicia sewed a pink dress with a triangle, a circle, a rectangle and a square on the front for Adaora. Then she made an embroidered shirt and shorts for me.

Now Adaora likes eating paw-paw on her favourite plate, and triangles are her favourite shape. The trouble is, she loves her new pink dress so much that she won't wear anything else. So that's something new for me to worry about!